PLANNER

90

DAYS TO

SUCCESS

Start your new chapter of life !
Not tomorrow ! Not After ! Now !
Dream big, Play big, Win big!
Stay Focused, and be Unstoppable.
Have an Inspiring 'Why'
Stay Consistent ! And Trust the Process.

ISBN – 979 - 8729400423

GAME GAME GAME GAME
GAME GAME GAME
GAME GAME GAME
GAME GAME GAME
GAME GAME GAME

IT'S YOUR GAME.

START IT NOW

NOW NOW NOW NOW
NOW NOW NOW NOW
NOW NOW NOW NOW
NOW NOW NOW NOW
NOW NOW NOW

This Planner
Belongs To

AFFIRMATIONS

DAY 00

VISIONS

NOW NOW NOW **DAY 1** NOW
TODAY

DATE :

DAY 2
IS WHAT SEPARATES
THE BEST FROM THE REST!

DATE :

DAY 3

WORK WORK WORK

DATE :

DAY 4

IT'S YOUR MIND THAT YOU HAVE TO CONVINCE!

DATE :

TRUST THE PROCESS

DATE :

DAY 6
KEEP WORKING EVEN WITH ZERO RESULTS !

DATE :

DAY 7

KEEP WORKING HARD

DATE :

DAY 8

DON'T IGNORE YOUR OWN POTENTIAL

DATE :

NEVER LET
YOUR FEAR DECIDE

DATE :

DAY 10

STAY CONSISTENT

DATE :

SCARED ? .... GOOD !

DATE :

DAY 12

WE DON'T GROW WHEN WE STAY INSIDE OF OUR COMFORT ZONE

DATE :

STOP WAITING FOR TOMORROW! START NOW

DATE :

DAY 14

CHALLENGE YOU !
CHANGE YOU!

DATE :

_____

_____

_____

_____

_____

_____

_____

_____

_____

_____

_____

_____

_____

_____

_____

_____

DON'T WISH FOR IT

DATE :

DAY 16

WORK FOR IT!

DATE :

_____

_____

_____

_____

_____

_____

_____

_____

_____

_____

_____

_____

_____

_____

_____

_____

LEVEL UP!

DATE :

_____

_____

_____

_____

_____

_____

_____

_____

_____

_____

_____

_____

_____

_____

_____

_____

_____

_____

DAY 18

SEE YOURSELF AS A WINNER, PERFORM AS A WINNER

DATE :

NEXT LEVEL !

DATE :

_____
_____
_____
_____
_____
_____
_____
_____
_____
_____
_____
_____
_____
_____
_____
_____
_____

DAY 20

BE BOLD ... !

DATE :

_____

_____

_____

_____

_____

_____

_____

_____

_____

_____

_____

_____

_____

_____

_____

_____

DAY 21

HERE YOU WILL NOT SEE
BIG RESULTS! KEEP WORKING

DATE :

ATER 21 DAYS !
THE HABIT IS INSTALLED.
WHERE ARE YOU NOW?

_____

_____

_____

_____

_____

_____

_____

_____

_____

_____

_____

_____

_____

_____

NEXT CHAPTER OF YOUR LIFE IS STARTING !
WHAT IS YOUR STRATEGY FOR NEXT FEW 21 DAYS ?

_____

_____

_____

_____

_____

_____

_____

_____

_____

_____

_____

_____

_____

_____

_____

_____

DAY 22
KEEP GRINDING !

DATE :

NEVER LOSE THE WAY!

DATE :

DAY 24

KEEP YOUR BRAIN ACTIVE

DATE :

WORK SMART !

DATE :

DAY 26

KEEP GOING

DATE :

_____

_____

_____

_____

_____

_____

_____

_____

_____

_____

_____

_____

_____

_____

_____

_____

_____

YOUR ONLY LIMIT IS YOU

DATE :

DAY 28

HERE IS THE BIG CHANGE WHERE THE MAGIC HAPPEN

DATE :

GOOD THINGS TAKE TIME

DATE :

IF NOT NOW THEN WHEN

DATE :

YOU CAN SEE IT,
YOU CAN FEEL IT

DATE :

_____

_____

_____

_____

_____

_____

_____

_____

_____

_____

_____

_____

_____

_____

_____

DAY 32

EVERYDAY IS A NEW OPPORTUNITY

DATE :

IF YOU PLAY SMALL

DATE :

YOU STAY SMALL

DATE :

WAKE UP
WITH DETERMINATION

DATE :

DAY 36
KEEP GOING

DATE :

KEEP GRINDING

DATE :

BOOST ... !

DATE :

DO THE BEST !

DATE :

DAY 40

KEEP GRINDING

DATE :

DAY 41

THINGS START TO BE
STANDARDS ! NEVER STOP !

DATE :

MEASURE

ATER 41 DAYS !
WHERE ARE YOU NOW ?
WHAT ARE YOUR STRENGTHS ?

_____

_____

_____

_____

_____

_____

_____

_____

_____

_____

_____

_____

_____

_____

_____

WHAT ARE YOUR WEAKNESSES ? BUILD A PLAN !

_____

_____

_____

_____

_____

_____

_____

_____

_____

_____

_____

_____

_____

_____

_____

DAY 42

KEEP THE LEVEL UP !

DATE :

LEVEL UP! LEVEL UP!

DATE :

DAY 44

KEY IS HARD WORK

DATE :

DON'T GIVE UP! NEVER!

DATE :

DAY 46

YOU MASTER YOURSELF!

DATE :

NEVER LOSE THE TARGET

DATE :

DAY 48
YOUR "WHY"

DATE :

HAVE A VISION

DATE :

_____

_____

_____

_____

_____

_____

_____

_____

_____

_____

_____

_____

_____

_____

_____

_____

_____

DAY 50

BELIEVE AND ACHIEVE

DATE :

IT ALL HAPPENS IN YOUR MIND

DATE :

DAY 52

UNLOCK IT IN YOUR
MIND TO ACHIEVE IT

DATE :

DAY 53

MAKE YOURESLEF PROUD

DATE :

_____
_____
_____
_____
_____
_____
_____
_____
_____
_____
_____
_____
_____
_____
_____
_____
_____
_____
_____

PLAY HARD !

DATE :

FOCUS ALL THE WAY!

DATE :

DAY 56

FOCUS ALL THE TIME!

DATE :

HAVE A STRATEGY

DATE :

IT'S YOUR GAME

DATE :

IT TAKES TIME!

DATE :

DAY 60

CHANGE THE PLAN

DATE :

_____

_____

_____

_____

_____

_____

_____

_____

_____

_____

_____

_____

_____

_____

_____

_____

NO SHORTCUTS!

DATE :

MEASURE

ATER 60 DAYS !
WHERE ARE YOU NOW ?
ENJOY AND TRUST THE PROCESS !

_____

_____

_____

_____

_____

_____

_____

_____

_____

_____

_____

_____

_____

_____

_____

_____

TWO MONTHS OF GRINDING !
KEEP GRINDING !

_____

_____

_____

_____

_____

_____

_____

_____

_____

_____

_____

_____

_____

_____

DAY 62

ONLY HARD WORK

DATE :

_____

_____

_____

_____

_____

_____

_____

_____

_____

_____

_____

_____

_____

_____

_____

MAKE A BREAK

DATE :

DAY 64

NEVER QUIT

DATE :

MAKE IT HAPPEN !

DATE :

DAY 66
STAY POSITIVE

DATE :

DEDICATION

DATE :

DAY 68

BEAST MODE

DATE :

DAY 69

EXECUTE ... !

DATE :

DAY 70

EVERYTHING IS UNDER CONTROL

DATE :

NEVER CHANGE THE TARGET

DATE :

DAY 72

DON'T TELL ABOUT YOUR PLANS

DATE :

FOCUS !

DATE :

DAY 74

NO UNCONSCIOUS MODE!
ALWAYS BRAIN OPEN!

DATE :

BRAIN ON!

DATE :

_____
_____
_____
_____
_____
_____
_____
_____
_____
_____
_____
_____
_____
_____
_____
_____

NEAR TO FINISHED LINE ?
THIS IS A MARATHON WITHOUT
ANY FINISHED LINE !

_____

_____

_____

_____

_____

_____

_____

_____

_____

_____

_____

_____

_____

_____

_____

_____

THE MORE YOU PROGRESS ON THIS MARATHON, THE MORE YOU WIN!

DAY 76

KEEP GRINDING

DATE :

YOUR DESERVE IT!

DATE :

DAY 78

PLAY ALWAYS FOR THE FIRST PLACE!

DATE :

THE TOP!

DATE :

DAY 80

KEEP THE HABIT, TO HAVE IT!

DATE :

DAY 81

PLAY BIG ... WIN BIG

DATE :

DAY 82

HIGH SPEED, TO SUCCEED

DATE :

LET RESULTS SPEAK!

DATE :

DAY 84

DON'T WISH FOR IT!

DATE :

HUSTLE!

DATE :

DAY 86

PAIN IS TEMPORARY!

DATE :

_____
_____
_____
_____
_____
_____
_____
_____
_____
_____
_____
_____
_____
_____
_____
_____

PUSH HARD!

DATE :

DAY 88
KEEP GRINDING AND NEVER STOP

DATE :

KEEP BOOTING!

DATE :

DAY 90

NEVER STOP !

DATE :

CONFIRMATIONS

A MUST

THINGS I WILL ACHIEVE

Habit : _____

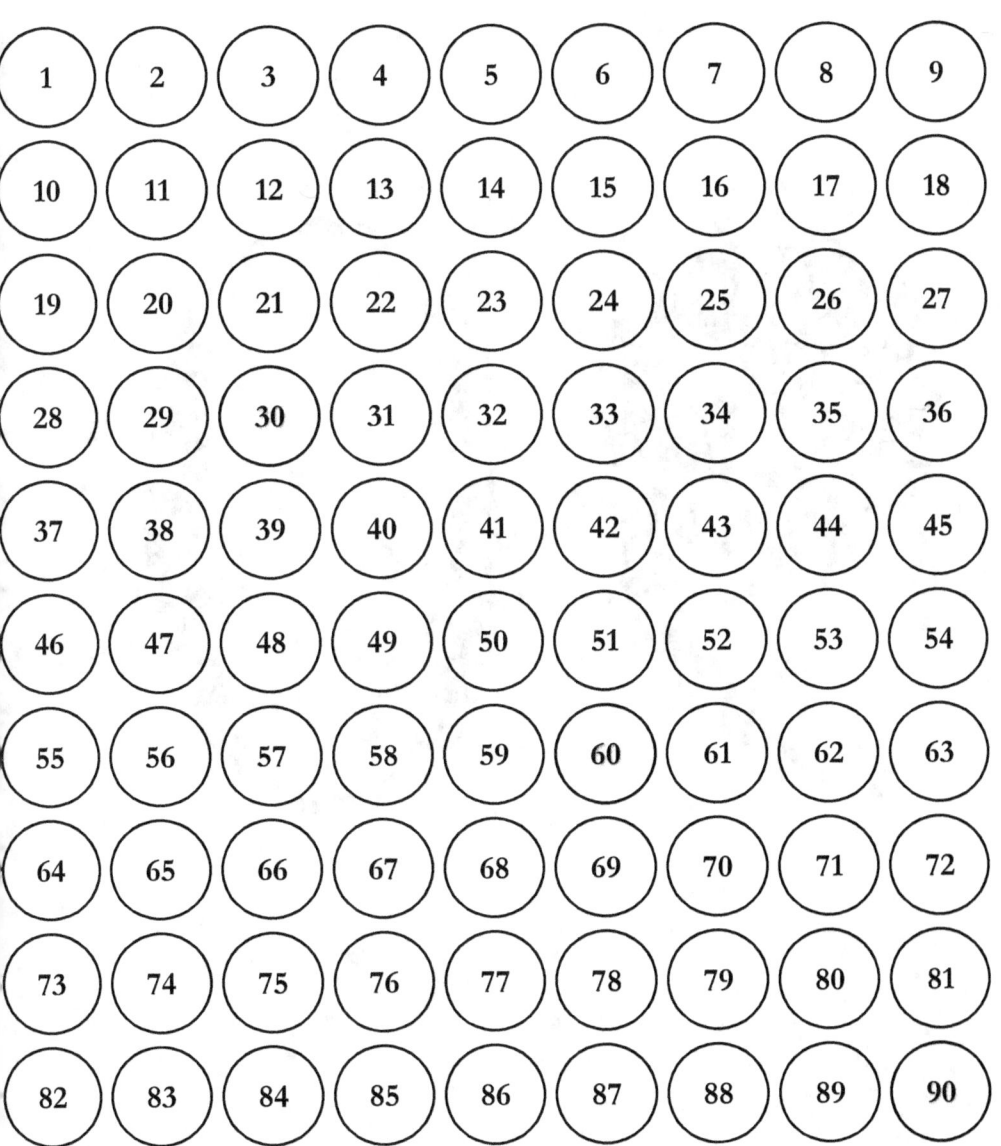

Result : _____

Never Quit